there goes
the neighborhood
™

Other Andrews and McMeel books from The Neighborhood:

Sound Sleeping in The Neighborhood

The Neighborhood in Color

High Stepping Through The Neighborhood

there goes the neighborhood

T.M.

by Jerry Van Amerongen

Andrews and McMeel
A Universal Press Syndicate Company
Kansas City • New York

ISBN: 0-8362-1874-4

Library of Congress Catalog Card Number: 90-85472

Preface

Hello Dear Reader!

This is the last full-size book collection of The Neighborhood that will be published. No, my publisher isn't mad at me. . .at least I don't think so! If you're not aware, I stopped drawing The Neighborhood this past July (July 28, 1990, to be exact). It had been syndicated in a goodly number of this country's more discriminating newspapers since October 1980.

Why did I discontinue The Neighborhood? . . . Well, it had nothing to do with that business about the women's shoes. The primary reason for discontinuing The Neighborhood was creative in nature. I felt there was a real possibility of going stale if I didn't move on to something new, something that would keep my interest up and my creative sap flowing.

I wanted to stop work on The Neighborhood while it still had honest energy and vitality—and while I was still getting a kick out of doing it.

In addition, there were certain aspects of cartooning which I didn't have the opportunity to work with—the idea of recurring characters, for example. I wanted to see what it was like to develop gags within the framework of specific personalities . . .to write for specific characters.

I also wanted to take a run at drawing a strip cartoon (multiple panels) as opposed to the single-panel format of The Neighborhood. I thought this would be a challenge, and it is! I thought recurring characters presented in a strip format would add texture and depth to the kind of humor I'd employed in The Neighborhood.

You may want to keep your eyes peeled, because I've been working on a new strip called Ballard Street, which takes a selected group of the folks you often see in The Neighborhood and settles them along a one-block stretch of this street. (Actually, Ballard Street is the name of the street I grew up on.) It should begin popping up in newspapers in March of 1991. Hopefully it will come to a paper near you. If it doesn't, perhaps you and your friends could organize an unruly, torch-carrying mob.

For now, though, I'd like to say I'm proud of the work I've done on The Neighborhood. I would like to take this opportunity to say thank you for your interest in my work—I very much appreciate it—and for buying this book. . .you are buying this book aren't you? I'd also like to thank each of you who took the time to write over the years. . .I've saved five of the seven letters, and now have them framed in my dining room.

—Jerry Van Amerongen
February 1991

"Impostor" is the word that creeps into
Mr. Markey's mind.

Regarding the idea that evolution may soon rob us of
our eyebrows . . . Gregory has himself
a good little chuckle.

The Henry Sturgis Power Hanky.

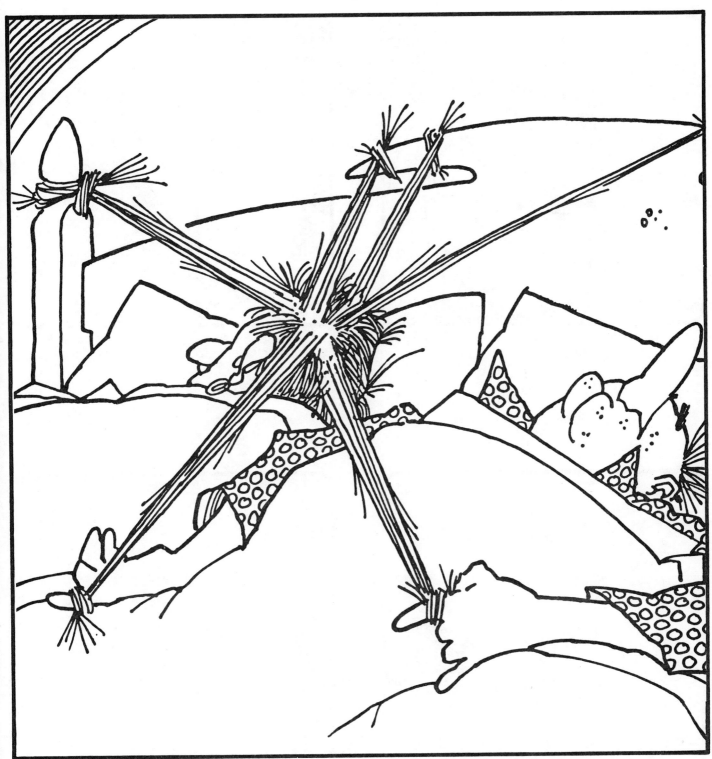

Brian spends a restless night dreaming about tying down furniture he has to move.

Over at the Plumbing Federation, contractors wish for good luck.

Another Personality Test that's managed to substantiate Morton's bent towards cynicism.

The sculpture is entitled, "Imperiled."

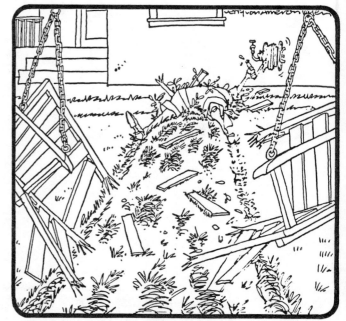

The folks at the Zippy Recoil Hose Co. are gonna hear from Sherman Briggs.

The Rodeo Bar & Grill tests the boundaries of theme coordination.

Graham figures it out.

Harold spends some quality time with his new pants.

Another bummer day for Neal.

Once again the story line begins its predictable drift toward our feathered barnyard friends.

Waiting begins to take its toll on Arnie.

Remember when knowing your sign used to be enough?

Aaron is about to blow the curve on the Floral Carbon opinion survey.

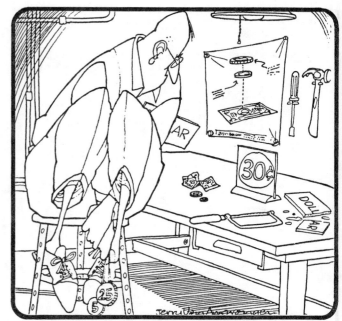

The notion of "30 cents on the dollar" continues to tweak Ray's imagination.

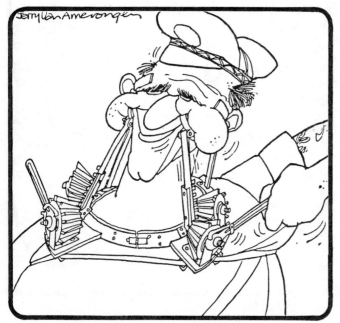

Capt. Kerby screws his face into a broad, albeit forced, smile.

Early on, the Gods of Inadequacy ganged up on Howie.

John would appear to be propelled by the
simpler things of life.

Carson pinpoints the unusual aftertaste.

Gloria maced her only serious competitor.

Unlike her husband, Clair isn't waiting for the next
good thermal.

Carolyn finally locates Bob.

Kenneth clears out the after-lunch cobwebs.

Picnicking on Worrisome Point.

What if the cows did come home . . .

Betsy's fascinated by things that frighten her.

Leaving Paul with a punch bowl is like leaving an explosives expert alone with a bridge support.

Oh, oh. Connie's in the wildflowers again.

Conrad is of the Free Association school.

Clifford is about to learn the extent of Mr. Spivey's space requirements.

Paul's paintings are born of apprehension.

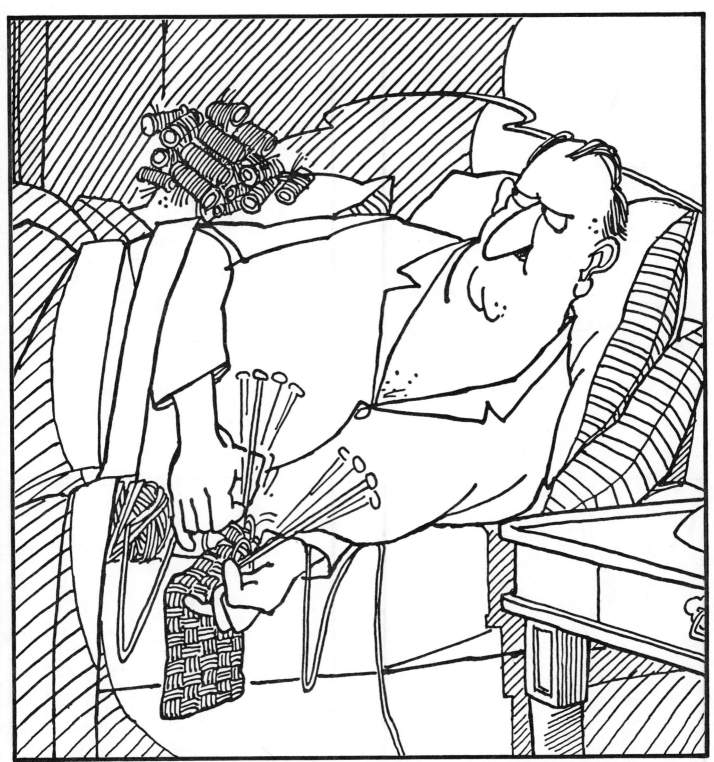

Although he's gotten more in touch with his feminine side, George remains private about it.

It's easy to see why Barry likes to live within walking distance of work.

At home with the Lone Ranger.

Last night Nolan dreamt his competitors had begun disguising themselves as cheap lawn furniture!

Christina adds density to her cake.

An impending coincidence.

Colleen remains Charles' first line of defense against reality.

Clifford attempts to diffuse a potentially emotional situation.

Another bad year at the Burpey Toy Company.

Gary is not a likely candidate for a power breakfast.

It's easy to see why the gymnastics team of Jocko and Boveen have turned to a life of crime.

Paul dabbles with self-expression.

It's entirely the wrong shirt for Bobby to be wearing.

Mr. Carson strictly adheres to time management.

Artie earned his merit badge in Crowd Control.

Dick's a man who knows his hose.

Another good reason not to wear baggy pants.

Carol enlightens Ken.

Spying a crowded intersection ahead,
Colin pretends to take a call.

It's the pea thing that casts Bernie in the role of solitary diner.

Phyllis is new to the position.

Another couple with too much free time.

Marchell is about to walk away with the Pet Trainer of the Year Award.

Bob is a contingency advocate.

Meanwhile, over at the Bakery Workers' Retirement Center . . .

Bill's Weed Eater becomes a tweed eater.

Inanimate objects confound Uncle Bosco.

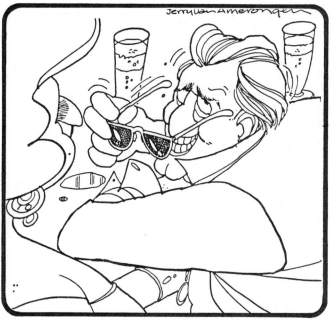

Randy sheds the ceremonial garb of indifference.

Adventurer Daryl Chambers at the laundromat.

The Acme Block and Tackle Company's
annual picnic.

So! The disagreement continues.

Connie's body is a vessel of inefficient motion.

Another troublesome day at the office.

The raft brings a constant pressure to Bill's life.

Gesundheit!

Celeste is not without her issues.

This wouldn't appear to be the day Russell goes out and gets that new job.

Capt. Bob breaks loose from his moorings.

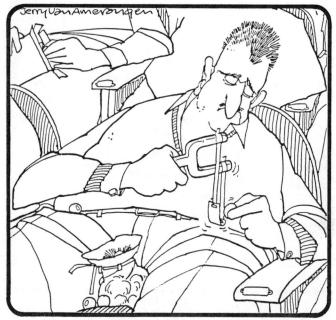

Carl responds to the idea of sitting through commercials at the movies.

Dinsdale underestimates the sophistication of his sales force.

The Carlisles own a small vicious dog.

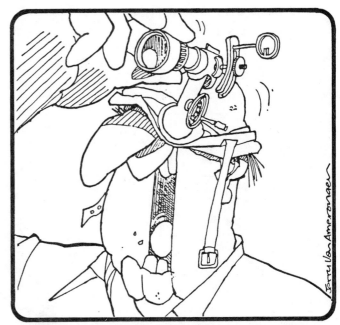

Berry has a nodding acquaintance with reality.

Curly is a man's man.

"I see you're a family man, Mr. Chambers."

How we choose a president.

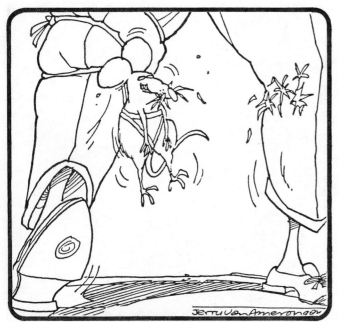

Bob hits upon a plan to affect a more manly,
wide-legged gait.

The last time Gary had this many drinks, tiny
amphibians fell on his head.

Clifford reacts badly to the idea of containment.

". . . Then, of course, there's this problem with the wheel."

As a first step, Alex is going to cancel Uncle Basco's subscription to *Mower Monthly*.

Elliot is a sort of lightning rod for throw rugs.

Berry's all but given up on the squirrel problem.

Bob gets off his high horse.

Creative person searching for ideas.

Here's how it works. You may choose to drop any one of your three rides from your "final points" total.

Bob watches as his cycle of nesting is broken.

Brad and Winnie have been together for a long time.

Bob's day brightens considerably.

Cliff is one of your no-frills caretakers.

Garrett is a functionalist, who owns a glass table.

Winter tip: Don't leave home with damp clothing.

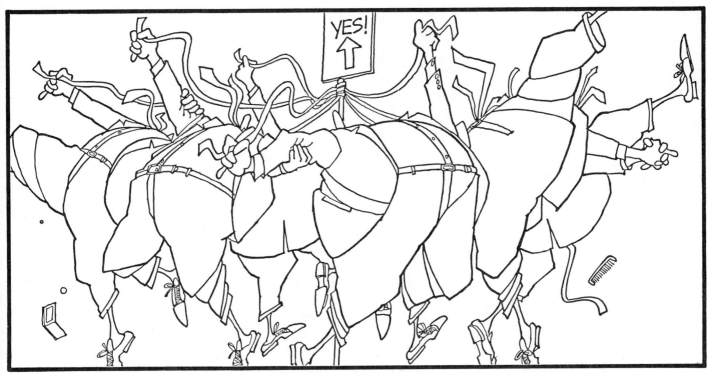

Citing increased quarterly profits since the noontime gatherings began, the management team continues to meet.

The Camera Owners with Self-timers Club.

The movie-goer in front of Ben pays the price for maintaining a perfectly erect posture.

Adage Amour: If it works, don't fix it.

Ah, the day-to-day joys of a telecommunications
enthusiast.

Elliot doesn't come naturally to the business.

Avant guard.

Gil was suddenly sorry he used the phrase "beat it."

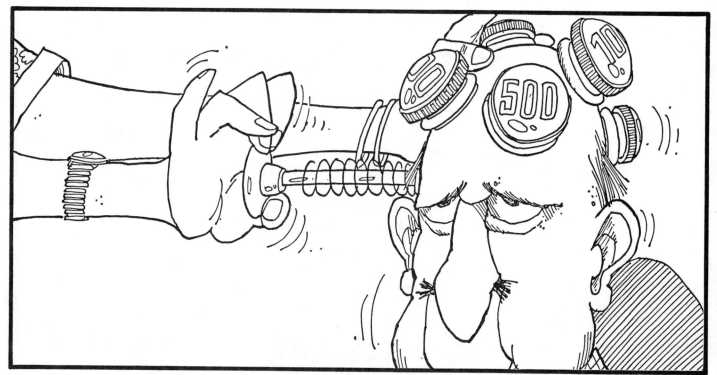

Does your thought process sometimes feel like this?

Berry's about to get some relief from that annoying back itch.

Irony . . . or was it?

The seamy side of naval retirement.

The day Barry's dad lost his job.

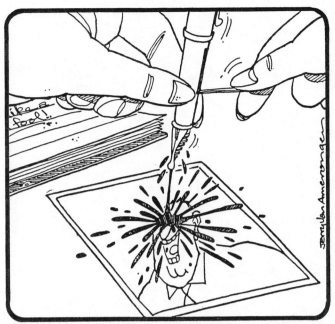

Carol's disagreement with Bob extends well into her journaling time.

First, get your audience's attention.

Before and after Archie Snaps' power play.

Smitty (Big Deal) Arbuckle and that stupid
paper clip of his.

Bar owner and naturalist Gregory Smyth Evers.

The Fencing Federation likes to discourage
spontaneous celebrations.

Two fiancés and another guy.

Kenny builds a sort of shrine to his latest interest.

Business promotion gives way to road hazard.

Mr. Gregory fancies himself a bit of an entertainer.

Chuckie has emancipation issues.

Herb continues his provocative ways.

Carla messes up.

Over at the Men's Athletic and Social Club.

At the mouth of Chortle Cavern.

Well, of course, the duck went nuts.

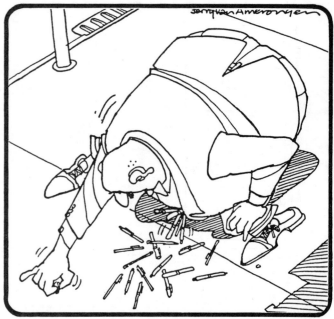

A writer bending over.

Another morning without toast.

"And, of course, the fish is always fresh."

Alice has a callous disregard for Philip's space.

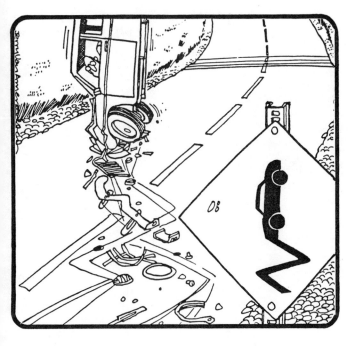

Eric steps out of a biting wind.

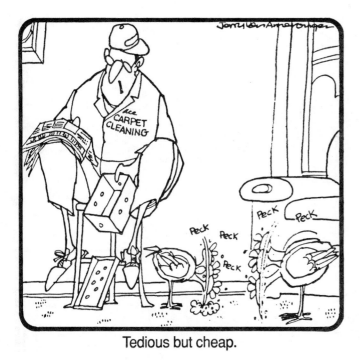

Tedious but cheap.

Bugs for Peace.

ACE
PARTY RENTAL

GALA EVENT PLANNING

How our brain loses things along the way.

Helen strikes back.

Rosco's dog remains inexplicably drawn to facial hair.

Brad's struggle with vanity continues.

"Yoo-hoo, Philip. I got more aspirin!"

"Gracie quit."

"Two times, Herbert. I only asked you to get me water two times."

Bonnie is beginning to view Powell as a traffic bump on her road to love.

Movies are sometimes suddenly compelling.

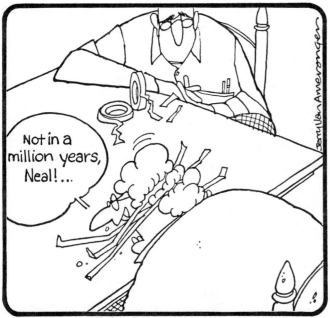

Meanwhile, Neal hasn't gotten the apology he's been looking for.

Bob's Family Systems Early Warning Signal kicks in.

Birdie and Paul have no idea how they affect others.

Mr. Bixby puts a stop to another misdirected presentation.

Bennett's thoughts turn to his neighbor.

"Then can we call the plumber?"

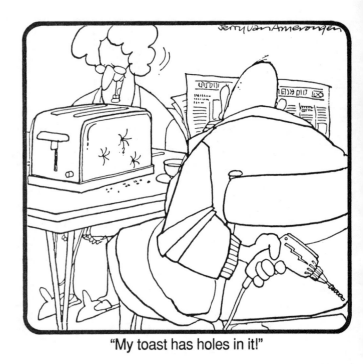

"My toast has holes in it!"

Raymond decides to lie as quietly as possible.

An abuse of small-engine technology.

This wouldn't appear to be one of Miss Stacy's more stable days.

Glenn is pulled along in the slipstream of Beverly's life.

Bad news for the folks in the next apartment. Morgan's a real homebody.

Time to clip those nails, thought Roy.

Gary sees his chance for a settee.

A dab of glue keeps kitty from underfoot.

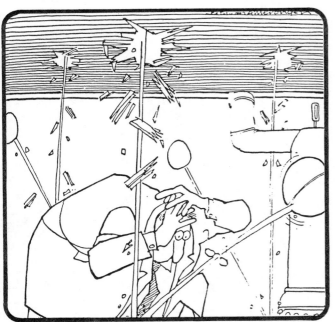

In the basement of the Slam Dunk Training Center.

Philip had been one of the very first to arrive.

Animal trainer extraordinaire, Franklin Hodges, causes a stir among the skaters.

Alex approaches his reading in a communal spirit.

That great meat tenderizer called life is making progress with Clarence.

Colin is flushed from the protective pocket of indifference.

A more contrite Godzilla.

"The folks down at the Pringle Nut and Bolt Company are gonna hear about this."

Higgins' mistake was firing his pitching coach while he still had access to the pitching machine.

Uncle Bosco makes a mockery of the Horned Hats Contest.

"Maurice will be your waiter."

oh, such a perfect place to gaze upon Mr. Dopey-face!

Poet and thrill seeker Wayne Chambers.

The years have been a lesson to Bobby Lee.

Philip's a man who keeps his own counsel.

Richie finally gets the girl to make eye contact.

Another failure to thoroughly synchronize
athletic activities.

To get a bench to himself, all Eugene has to do is point.

Breakfast becomes an event of some consequence
for Bob.

The dicey business of dressing up for lawn work.

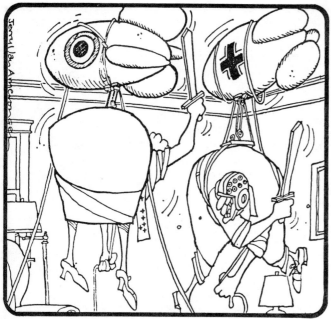

. . . As the winter months drag on.

No wonder my salary is chicken feed, thought Ted.

A life of indecision catches up with Marcus.

No wonder some men are skittish about
showing affection.

"I pretty much hate the veterinary business, Alice."

Hamsters prove equally unstable as
explosives carriers.

Announcing winners at the Excavators
Awards Dinner.

It's one of Ken's favorite spots.

Meanwhile, at Chuck's Crayfish Emporium, they've taken the theme angle as far as they can.

Brad experiences a surge of reluctance.

Connie and Tom like their new dresser.

Garrett is faced with a whole new reality.

So begins another failed attempt.

Enjoying the Happy Meal Deal down at
the steakhouse.

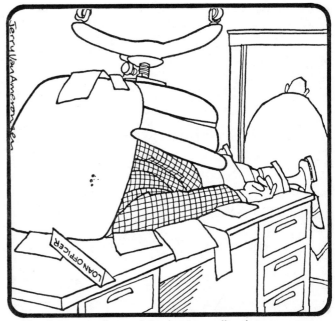

Charles soon tires of the loan-application process.

Gregory experiences occasional bouts
of omnipotence.

Carl's thinking about making the switch to Diet Coke.

Philip's painting, "Two Dobermans and a Bunny," runs into early problems.

Clifford's life is a roller coaster.

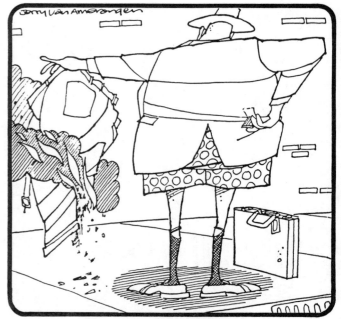

Risk taker Garrett O'Malley.

Gloria applies her perfume.

"The dog wants out, Gracey."

Gerald couldn't have been more pleased.

Eric's interest in birds dovetails nicely with his interest in soup.

"Albert, will you see that Mr. Mimms gets more of the Linguini a la Milanese."

Another incredibly literal person.

Mr. Barney joins his wife on the porch.

Cinching is no cinch for Curley.

Used-car dealer housebreaking his pet.

Claire searches for a deeper meaning.

Another foreshortened playtime for Stinky
(the butcher's son).

Gregory rewards himself for putting in a
productive morning.

OK, so it doesn't look like a fox from here, but Bob is intrigued just the same.

"Make that two Milk-Bones, Harriet."

There's always someone around who will oblige you.

Whether one enjoys reading reports has a lot to do with HOW one reads them.

Mr. Hewitt possesses a nurturing management style.

There's no such thing as just tagging along with Brad.

The folks at the Fish Market try to anticipate newly acquired tastes.

Berry, Gary and Larry, the Lurch Brothers.

Norbie is the steadying influence on the board.

Curtis is a stickler for realism.

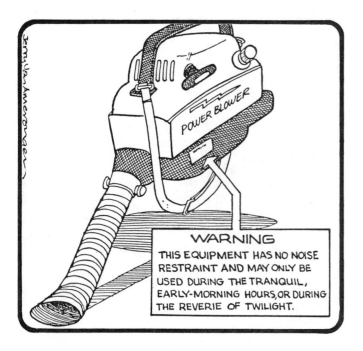

"Might we have a word with you in the office, Mr. Burphey. . ."

Wishing to maintain a manly presence at the Muffin Parlor, Carl rejects his cutesy glass.

It wouldn't be inappropriate to question Nelson's work ethic.

Another sign of mild unreality.

Living art.

Eric's literal mind-set is again in evidence.

Berry's toying with the idea of getting a dog.

It's not what you say; it's how you say it.

The room had an ocean view after all.

Businessman doing yardwork.

. . . And so the long trek toward the first hole begins.

Skipper adds a note of authenticity to
Bob's costume.

A disturbing chain of events.

"First time? . . ."

Time to eliminate the company specialist,
thought Mr. Pringle.

At home with Bucky and Captain Withers.

Cornell sings the fertility song.

The grueling business of tax avoidance.

The actual presentation of the pot roast brought an end to Philip's culinary critique.

Gil continues to spurn store-bought trimmers.

Margaret is to the Queen Anne what Ed is to the footstool.

When one reaches higher levels of management,
it doesn't necessarily mean one reaches
higher levels of consciousness.

For collectors of sock swatches, it's not the WHY
that's important, it's the HOW.

Mr. Giddings is well on his way to losing his aura
of leadership.

Chef Larry chafes under the yoke of Muzak.

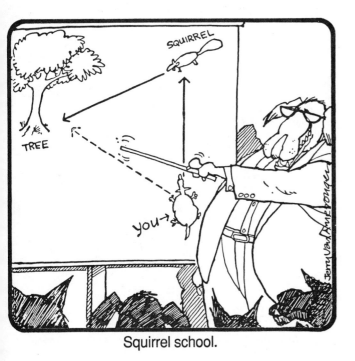

Squirrel school.

Gordon's in a contact mode.

"Would I be meeting with a fellow cat fancier, Mr. Carlisle?!"

"I take it, sir, you'd like us to massage the numbers a little more."

Orville's gonna get a stepladder first thing
in the morning.

The evening soon gives way to free-floating hostility.

TRIPLICATES: A confused sign painter, a
seldom-used waiting room, an obedient individual.

Cynthia appears to have fared better during
today's couples' counseling session.

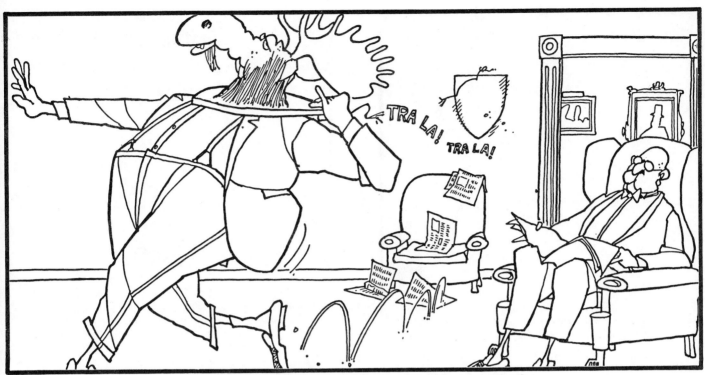

Is nothing sacred over at the Order of the Moose Lodge?

Happy birthday, Biffy.

Gwen's idea of a tidy camp site includes waterbugs.

Gary has so much trouble making decisions he almost never changes lanes.

The only real exercise Cliff gets is putting on his socks.

Connie always lets Glen know if she's happy.

Never break off a long-term relationship at the top of the stairs.

Ah, yes, that old love/hate thing with jellyrolls.

Mr. Carlisle maintains a proper countenance.

Since Charles embraced lawn sculpture, relations with his wife have improved markedly.

Kevin finds the little French sandwiches are a perfect accompaniment to inane party banter.

"Gesundheit . . ."

The ever-optimistic Eddie Spalding.

. . . and so another mating dance begins.

Gary gives himself over to the entertainment aspects
of his local news.

If Freddie were a tree, he'd be described
as having a shallow root system.

"Carlos, if you have concerns about the support you've received regarding Mr. Tuttle's distributor cap,
step in and discuss them."

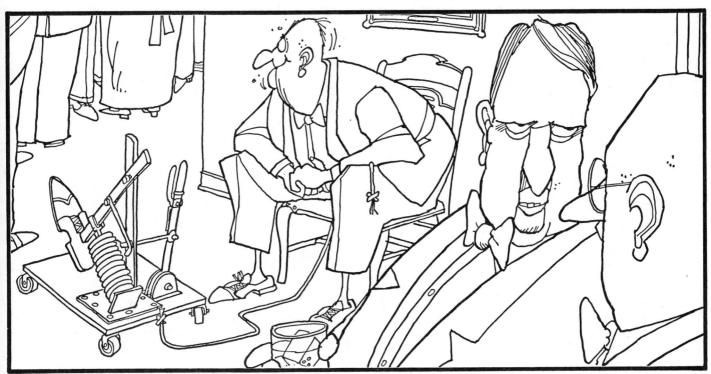

"Don't even look like you're thinking of bending over."

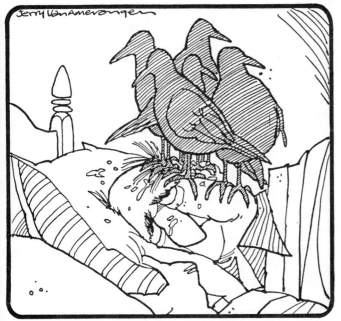

Gil Sturgis went on to write such books as *Crow Lover No More* and *Beyond Feather Bedding*.

Occasionally Gordon identifies what he considers to be an idea.

Mrs. Giddings possesses an exaggerated
sense of responsibility.

Sybil sets her typing aside to better respond to her
boss's latest crisis.

The Frantic Institute lets out.

Gloria hits on a bold, new plan to outflank the bar scene.

More than one of the local girls saw herself as the Lawn Queen.

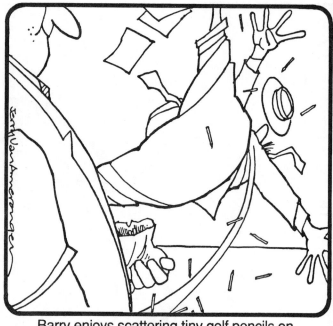

Barry enjoys scattering tiny golf pencils on hard surfaces.

Congratulations! You've succeeded in making your twice-baked potatoes less edible than the packing material around them.

You call that sarcasm?

Meanwhile, over at the Sarcasm Write-off.

I believe my portion is larger... more generous, if you will.

A classy little troublemaker.

Garrett lost his footing some time back.

Merle has drainage issues.

"Just fell the thing, Steve."

You can bet the bear wasn't.

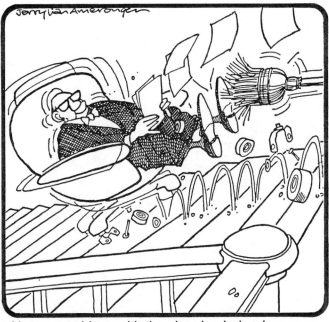

Never get chippy with the cleaning lady when your office is at the head of the stairs.

The long-suffering wife of kiddie comic Shelly Ligget.

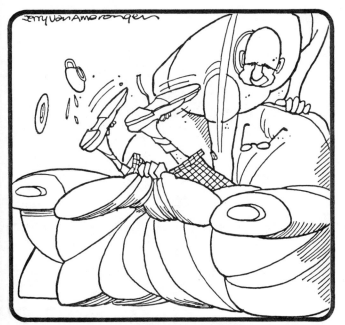

Reggie believes the secret to conflict resolution is to firmly lock your elbow.

Max is the kind of guy who likes to make efficient use of his time.

"No more head-butting, young man!"

Standing at the ragged edge of thought.

Not just another pretty haircut.

Sammy's in the process of quitting.

It was, for Paul, a compelling thought.

It's the acrobats from upstairs.

Biff is the more optimistic of the two.

Moonlighting mason.

When withdrawing from one group to another,
Bob takes pains to avoid hurt feelings.

Rex heads across the street, thus perpetuating a
medical supplier's dream.

Neal reminds himself not to come this way
on Mondays.

Carpet cleaning by the lowest bidder.

Big Louie's too big for the business.

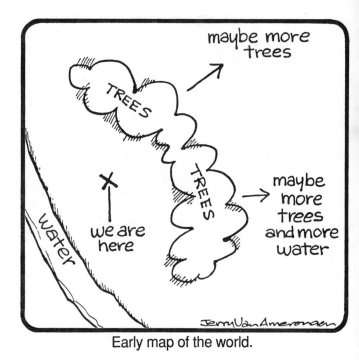

Early map of the world.

Occasionally some of Jason's body parts fall into disharmony with other parts.

". . . and, of course, the step-in snare is one of the easiest traps to conceal."

It's always something at the drive-up mailbox.

Brian likes to direct his thinking.

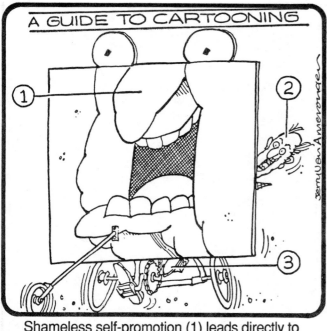

Shameless self-promotion (1) leads directly to
Bob's (2) ankle problems (3).

"Graham used to be a minor-league outfielder."

Bob feels so responsible, he refrains from going out
in public for fear he wouldn't be able to adequately
assist others in an emergency.

The guy whose job it is to think up macho situations
for TV beer commercials.

It's never really high tea with Uncle Felix.

A group of pained outsiders.

A long, tedious winter lies ahead for Marcy.

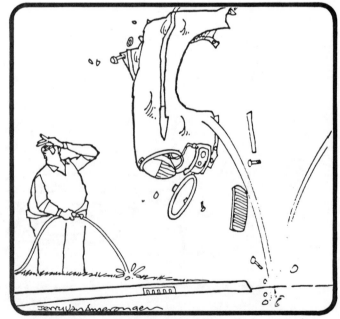

Barry gets an indication that his wife is returning from the store.

Uncle Fred hates it when the dog from upstairs gets out.

The truth is like a shadowy movement on the very periphery of Garrett's consciousness.

you could call me during the day to say I love you... you could be more attentive to my needs...you could buy me presents...

Mr. Barney continues to do penance well into the evening.

SHOO, SHOO, YOU NASTY SQUIRREL!

Miss Maybell is very protective of Spot's territorial needs.

No eggs this morning.

Uncle Ben and Bucky.

Alex is always working on himself.

Pencil

Professional instincts are aroused within housing inspector Jennings.

Ed's been at the strobe-light factory now for 13 years.

Though he couldn't have known at the time, Bruce was the first to learn of Mr. Springer's fledgling experiments with flight.

Philip continues to suppress his feelings.

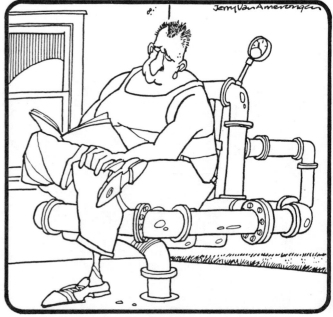

On the patio with pipe fitter George Tinker.

The comedy of life punctuated by the drama of life.

Gordon is awash with relief.

At home with a motivational enthusiast.

The allure was, of course, intense.

Carla's depth perception is such that she often mistakes bugs on the porch screen for birds in the backyard.

Cliff returns to his unique styling on the concertina, as Carol heads for another movie.

Fredrick worries about whether he should call someone about his worrying.

Spike wants to go, too.

"Mother's gone now, Arnold."

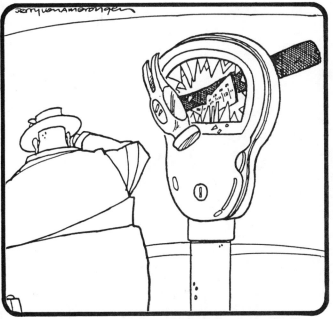

Having cost him two tickets in two days, Philip marks the meter for future reference.

Maintaining the larger-than-life sculpture of her ex-husband is a comfort to Nancy, especially after she finishes the paper.

Home videos.

". . . and, yes, a fussy eater as well."

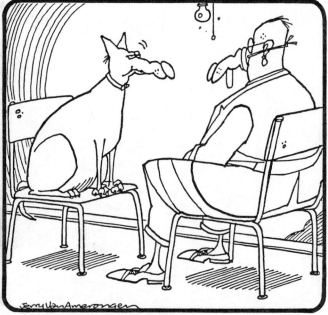

Another sign of Ben's flagging interest in society as a whole.

Another salesman totally overwhelmed by this year's sales theme.

Velma's spent a good deal of her career in ham-and-eggers.

Timing remains an essential part of the Burphy Brothers' routine.

"Do you think Jerry smeared you on purpose?
He's got a reputation to maintain, you know."

Gary forgets his paranoia long enough to identify
the hotel's hired killer.

Carl uses his own jack to see if his neighbor's car
alarm, which has been on for one hour and
forty minutes, might not be deactivated by
repositioning the vehicle.

While the kids encouraged Mom to take up a hobby,
they never dreamed she'd settle on mastering the
entire songbook of Iron Butterfly.

Unfortunately for Carl, Helen was in a fowl mood.

Pondering a poorly thought-out design concept.

Roscoe's tired of staying home alone.

It's the third try with the pleated shirt.

The product itself is incentive enough at the
Carlisle Typewriter Company.

Marian is fully capable of tinkering with an idea
long enough to make a mess of it.

Tony teeters on the edge of involvement.

Gary gets his hair moosed.

After today, painter Herb Nichols has vowed never to wear baggy, snaggable overalls and little Andy Prather has had the flared handlebars removed from his bike.

. . . and so, the forced march through life continues.

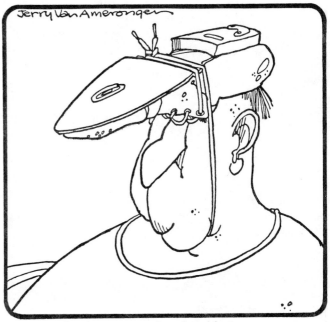

Cutting corners in a hard-hat area.

Cliff is one of your effortlessly harmonious people.

Clifford's a gaping receptacle for temptation.

Eddie's looking to enlarge upon a theme.

A man with no alternative plan.

There'll be no more "just slip this in with the rest" projects today.

Gordon tends to be influenced by the most dominant element in his surroundings.

One day out and already a snag.

"Let's see if we can't get J.B. interested in bow ties."

Last night was a lot tougher on Benny
than he thought.

Another neighborhood with a warped value system.

The prophetic nature of fortune cookies.

Another Monday.

Tom takes a fateful turn toward ambivalence.

And so it goes over at the Hockey Players
Retirement Center.

Bob likes to give the illusion of urgency.

A tough neighborhood.

The encroachment of adhesives on the fabric of the family.

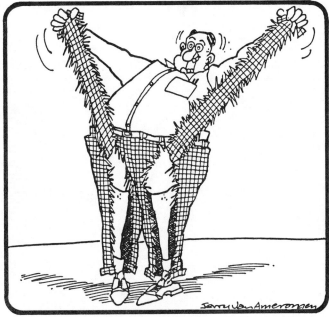

Looking into Jeffrey's motivations is like looking into an empty room.

Seeing his sales pitch falling on deaf ears, Randall decides to make a preliminary close.

Berry's been watching too many old cartoons.

For once artistic expression overcomes crass commercialism.

Could Nancy be anymore deprived of
natural instincts?!

"Bob and Marcia seem to be cultivating an
interest in fish."

The next ball up in the great pinball game of life.

A salad slinger . . . but why, wondered Marcia.

Oooh, such a pretty, pretty little lady!... Mommy's pretty, pretty, pretty lady!

Notes from Key West: The Hemelshots are again reminded of the dangers of taking early retirement.

Notes from Key West: Thad and Hillary sow the seeds of discontent.

Notes from Key West: The gulf between tourist and native.

Notes from Key West: Leaving everything for a T-shirt shop in the islands provides little salve for Ed's mid-life struggle.

"Never mind, Clark, it wasn't the tap dancers from upstairs."

Another perfectly compatible couple.

"Tomorrow, how about I slip out and get a flyswatter . . ."

The deeper effects of Jason's layoff are becoming evident to others.

Stephen stays within striking distance of hard work.

Gordon remains remarkably unaware of his surroundings.

It's such a hassle to get a good idea.

Cliff struggles with a negative mind-set.

Bob is almost a very prophetic guy.

Gary spent a lot more time measuring material for the
bird suit than he did measuring the rope.

Another reason not to trust Ben with detail work is
that right now he thinks he's chasing
a common housefly.

Another overture from the meat industry representatives.

Gus reacts badly to sudden moves.

Raymond does a little mental roughhousing.

Technology goes right over Vivian's head.

It's 15-love over at Gene and Shirley's.

Tom slips into his dress pants.

You get the feeling Bob's not going out and grabbing life by the throat anytime soon.

Deep thinking screws up another perfectly nice day.

Gracie isn't above a little flash in the kitchen.

Larry's better at trimming than he is at fathering.

Compelling images come to Curtis, like chubby little kitties sitting on stubby little stools.

Gesundheit!

Felix presents himself at the pharmacy window.

Graham does some more intellectual posturing.

Having doubts about Brian as a husband, Cynthia wonders how he'd be as a ham sandwich.

Normally you wouldn't expect the pursuit of entomology to ruin a good set of shocks.

Philip has all but lost control of his department.

The low bidders.

Glenn drops all pretenses of sociability.

Mr. Harding tends to pitch out those things which
fail to advance the pleasure of his day.

Mr. Chandler expands his sphere of influence.

Graham senses a shift in the office power structure.

Is there anything Mr. Alexander isn't prepared for?

It's that exposed stairwell again!

Whatever possessed Howard to jump on the bed?

But is therapy really helpful to those close to the patient?

Brian consults his medium in the produce department.

Remember to keep billing concerns to yourself until after your lawn man has completed the job.

Gretchen's tea of choice is Constant Comment.

"I'm afraid, Mrs. Pringle, I've had a run of bad luck in your bathroom."

A cloud gathers on florist Huey Prather's horizon.

No wonder Skippy's front teeth are always green.

The comprehensive tour.

Ben gets more out of TV than most people.

Young Fedderman's got a lot to learn about delegating.

"I don't believe we have a book entitled *Learn to Land*."